WOODY
ALLEN
AT WORK

THE PHOTOGRAPHS
OF BRIAN
HAMILL

WOODY ALLEN
AT WORK

THE PHOTOGRAPHS
OF BRIAN
HAMILL

ESSAY BY CHARLES CHAMPLIN ■ SELECTION AND COMMENTARY BY DERRICK TSENG

HARRY N. ABRAMS, INC., PUBLISHERS

For my beautiful daughter Cara, with total unconditional love forever

B.H.

EDITOR: Diana Murphy
DESIGNER: Dana Sloan

Library of Congress Cataloging-in-Publication Data
Hamill, Brian.
  Woody Allen at work: the photographs of Brian Hamill / essay by
  Charles Champlin; selection and commentary by Derrick Tseng.
        p.   cm.
  Filmography: p.185
  Includes index.
  ISBN 0–8109–1957–5
  1. Allen, Woody—Pictorial works.
  2. Allen, Woody—Criticism and interpretation.
          I. Tseng, Derrick. II. Champlin, Charles, 1926– III. Title.
  PN1998.3.A45H35   1995
  791.43'092—dc20   94–48322

Published in 1995 by Harry N. Abrams, Incorporated, New York
A Times Mirror Company

Printed and bound in Japan

All black-and-white photographs were printed by Vincent Tcholakian
of Diana Custom Photo Lab, New York.

Page 1: Woody Allen with Mary Steenburgen, *Another Woman*
Pages 2–3: With Mia Farrow, *Shadows and Fog*
Pages 6–7: With Carlo Di Palma, *Shadows and Fog*
Page 10: With Barbara Hershey, *Hannah and Her Sisters*

CONTENTS

Most of the individuals I've grown to love and admire are real people who have had snags and potholes and derailments along their journeys through life—people who've picked themselves up off the canvas and would never throw in the towel. They are few and rare. My family—mother and father, brothers Denis, Pete, Joe, Johnnie, and Tommy, and my wonderful sister Kathleen—are among this special group.

So is Woody Allen.

Woody is one of the few people on the planet I would trust in a lifeboat. He is a *man*. He's also an artist and a very caring parent. I've had the privilege of knowing him and working with him since 1976. We have both witnessed major changes in our lives since then. We both became fathers and, although we've both experienced ups and downs in our personal lives, our shared laughter while hanging out, a mutual love of this city, and the work we do together have given us a shorthand, a bond, and a loyal code that resulted in a friendship. Two streetwise mugs from Brooklyn.

I've worked with many top directors on many movies, but Woody is unique. His endless drive for excellence pushes me to work at the top of my talent. I want to thank him for the work and the laughs and the inspiration he's given me in the movie business. But mostly, I want to thank him for his loyalty as my friend—we've had fun.

Brian Hamill
New York City, 1994

What can one say about Brian Hamill? If Damon Runyon were still alive he'd have a field day with him. As dyed-in-the-wool a New Yorker as you can get, Brian is the quintessential street character. Always the eyes are open to what's going on—who's on the hustle, who's on the make—what citizens look solid, which are clearly shady. His currency is knowledge, information, connections, street smarts. There's not a person he doesn't know or he doesn't have the skinny on or know about, not a restaurant, not a broad.—It's really quite astonishing. If ever the old joke applied—the one where the Pope is in New York and people ask, "Hey, who's the guy with Brian Hamill?" You want to know how to get to an obscure street in Chinatown? Ask Hamill.—Or the best place to eat in some godforsaken neighborhood in Brooklyn? He knows. He knows which actor is signed for which film before the actor knows and which round to bet which middleweight on which night because the fix is in. When we're filming on the streets of Manhattan there are always countless pedestrians who ogle the proceedings. Invariably they pay their respects to Brian; every out-of-work entertainer, every movie star, politician, athlete, and every beautiful woman. You always get the feeling Hamill and the passer-by are winking quietly as they say hello, both members of some inside fraternity.

It's that they trust him. They like him and trust him. He's honest, direct, an unadorned *mensch*. He's New York wise, tough, and to boot a great raconteur and mimic. I'd trust him with my kids' lives—on the other hand, if I needed someone to help me rob a bank I'd probably ask him first. So how can a guy raised in the tradition of the New York sidewalks and picking photography be anything but a sharpshooter? He's got eyes in the back of his head. He knows what shots are important and he gets them, plus he's got soul. Irish to the marrow, with all the artistic depth that that implies, Hamill is a mug who takes pretty pictures. He can compose, he can light, and he's to the point. He once told a producer who criticized the stills of his girlfriend for not making her beautiful enough, "I'm a photographer, not a magician." We've spent a lot of years together working the streets of this city and it's been a privilege.

Woody Allen

WOODY
ALLEN

THE
DIRECTOR
AT WORK

by Charles Champlin

Since 1965, when he wrote and appeared as a supporting player in the all-star farce *What's New Pussycat?*, Woody Allen has had a hand in thirty-one other films, twenty-six of which he wrote or co-wrote and directed, and in nineteen of which he has also acted, usually in the principal role. He even found time to write, direct, and star in some commercials for Italian television.

By any measure that is an extraordinary outpouring of creativity. No other American filmmaker in recent times has generated such a considerable body of work. Yet what is impressive and even historic about Woody Allen's achievement is not the quantity of the work but its quality and its uniqueness. Allen occupies a niche all by himself. He resembles no other filmmaker or actor; he is not almost like Jerry Lewis or Ingmar Bergman, François Truffaut or Federico Fellini or Alfred Hitchcock or anyone else, although he has admired them all, and Bergman is probably the filmmaker he respects above all others. Allen has matured into an *auteur* in the truest sense of the term, a writer-director whose films (even those he has co-written with others) carry his unmistakable signature on every frame.

His career offers a unique opportunity to follow a filmmaker's steep-rising curve of assurance and mastery, from early offerings that are little more than photographed jokes (marvelous jokes though they are) to films whose continually surprising diversity in form and intention, whose personal revelations and emotional force, and total, supple command of the resources of the medium place Woody Allen in the top rank of author-directors anywhere.

As he did when he was writing jokes and then doing stand-up comedy, he makes wonderful use of a surrealistic juxtaposing of ideas, breathtaking anachronisms, and inspired absurdities. In *Love and Death* (1975), set in the Russia of 1812 with the music of Prokofiev on the soundtrack, Diane Keaton at one point cries that man is created in God's image. Woody, wearing his contemporary horn-rims, says, "You think He wears glasses?" Keaton pauses a moment and murmurs, "Not with *those* frames."

His observations on what he finds bizarre and pretentious in the world enlivened the early films and they still do. In *Bananas* (1971), Howard Cosell and Don Dunphy broadcast a coup d'état in a fictional Central American country as if it were a sporting event, and Cosell lies beside the assassinated president in hopes of getting a few last gasping words. It is ridiculous, of course, but a wicked commentary on television's intrusive and deforming presence at real events.

Looking back over his films it is clear that *Annie Hall* in 1977, Woody's sixth film as a wholly independent writer-director with an unprecedented degree of autonomy, was a landmark and a turning point in his progress. For the first time he allowed himself to deal with his own professional and emotional experience. Alvy Singer is, as Allen had been, a stand-up comic working the college circuit and purporting to be a post-graduate neurotic deploying all the right code words from psychiatry and Comp. Lit. The jokes continue to be marvelous. What is to be made of a place, he asks of Los Angeles, whose contribution to culture is that you can turn right on a red light? It is a query that has gone into legend. Yet more and more the jokes are seen to be a transparent cover for Alvy's—Woody's—real concerns, including an abiding insecurity, heightened by the anti-Semitism he detects all about him in the society. There is rage and anxiety detectable beneath the jokes.

At that, the heart of the movie is the story of Alvy's love for Annie Hall—love found and then lost, but replaced in time by an enduring, understanding friendship. Alvy is at last mature enough to accept that beyond a relationship there can of course be hatred or despair but there can also be an ongoing affection strong enough to do anything except make the love affair work again.

Where memory leaves off and fiction begins in *Annie Hall* the viewer cannot say, but the Alvy-Annie romance, with its echoes of Allen and Keaton's own association, is so warmly charming and believable that the resonances can be felt. They helped bring *Annie Hall* its large commercial success and its sweep of the major Academy Awards. They also revealed an Allen willing and eager to draw on his emotions as well as his intellectual observations.

What could be noted in the film as well was Woody's growing confidence and skill as a filmmaker. *Annie Hall* is an exciting film visually as well as verbally, with moments that suggest a very special imagination at work. Woody as an adult sits in a grade school classroom surrounded by children, who are his classmates from childhood. He reminisces about them as they were (and as we see them), but in their childish voices they speak as the adults they became. "I'm into leather," says one of them boldly, and another admits to being a methadone addict.

It was on *Annie Hall* that Brian Hamill began his long and ongoing association as Allen's unit photographer, producing the revealing record of Woody at work to be seen in these pages. Hamill's timing could not have been better, because Allen was beginning the most significant and adventurous years of his career to date. The photographs confirm what was becoming clearer year by year: that Woody was not the nervously voluble neurotic of his stand-up comedy persona any more than Chaplin was the Little Tramp once out of camera range. The characterizations of the Tramp—and of Alvy and Woody's subsequent alter egos—may have been founded upon memory and experience, but they were conscious characterizations, enhancements upon elements of reality. In fact Woody is, as Chaplin was, a confident perfectionist running his show with a firm hand, sympathetic but aloof, as the photographs suggest.

Even before *Annie Hall* enjoyed its immense commercial popularity (immense by Allen's standards if not quite in the ballpark with *Terminator II*), he had written and was completing *Interiors* (1978), a film wildly different in tone from *Annie Hall*. It is a work of such darkly dramatic intensity, so unrelieved by a single joke, that it could very nearly be taken as coming from a different filmmaker altogether. Some viewers (and some critics) voiced an outraged sense of betrayal: Woody Allen was meant to be funny and had no right to be so serious. (He satirized the complaints two years later in *Stardust Memories*.) Yet seen now, in the context of all the later films, *Interiors* looks like a beginning rather than a detour, a declaration of creative independence rather than an aberrant indulgence. Allen was signaling he would not be typecast as a maker of comedies, and that instead he would set himself a fresh challenge each time out—in choice of tone, in technical problems to be conquered, in the comments he wants to make—as he has gone on to do.

Woody reveals in *Interiors* an ability to evoke sensitive and affecting performances from his cast, thus to generate an emotional impact beyond anything in his earlier work. The central performance by Geraldine Page is very affecting, and there are numerous splendid supporting performances, especially by Diane Keaton and Mary Beth Hurt as her daughters, E. G. Marshall as her ex-husband, and Maureen Stapleton as his new bride. Like Bergman and Jean Renoir, Allen demonstrates in *Interiors* a novelist's ability to analyze characters and relationships deeply.

As a director expanding his control of the medium's resources, he employs a muted, earth-toned palette and artfully austere set designs to enhance the somber mood of his film. Maureen Stapleton's appearance in a vivid red dress, the only splash of brightness in the film, becomes an exclamation point, defining by contrast the inhibited and unvoiced feelings that have afflicted everyone else until—pent-up emotions boiling over—the characters begin to say all the things that have been on their minds and roiling about in their souls. It is very much a proscenium drama, largely but not entirely indoors and looking forward to *September*, which takes place entirely inside one country house, under one roof.

In retrospect, even Woody might agree that he could have lightened up *Interiors* just a little. Yet the passage of time, and the revelations of the subsequent films, have been kinder to *Interiors* than were some of the critics of the moment. It is unquestionably a work of art—and unquestionably by Woody Allen.

Psychologists like to point out that we are everyone in our dreams. In the same sense, almost all writing (fiction and nonfiction) is in some way autobiographical, shaped by a life as lived, by remembered events, fears and feelings, thoughts, readings, friends, enemies, dreams, nightmares, hopes, and fancies. It is significant that the Allen films most successful with both critics and audiences are those that appear to have sprung most directly from his own life: experience as transmuted into fiction and charged with a truth of the spirit, though not following rote adherence to the facts.

When Woody at the end of *Manhattan* recites a litany of things that make life worth living and lists the graces of Willie Mays and the splendors of Mozart's *Jupiter* Symphony and Louis Armstrong's recording of "Potato Head Blues," there is little doubt the list is heartfelt, very personal.

Responding to the same autobiographical impulse that begat *Annie Hall*, he created *Manhattan* (1979) and *Stardust Memories* (1980). (His film-a-year creativity is still astonishing and he is customarily writing the next film while reshooting or doing final editing on the previous film.)

At one visually glorious level *Manhattan* is a celebration of the city Allen loves above all others: the Manhattan that embodied all his dreams and aspirations while he was growing up on the lower edges of the middle class across the river (but a world away) in Brooklyn. Manhattan was now his domain. Gordon Willis's sumptuous black-and-white cinematography tours the city's facades old and new while Tom Pierson's arrangements of George Gershwin tunes form the perfect musical accompaniment. The sequence, like the film as a whole, declares the director's growing confidence in his skills.

But *Manhattan* is not simply a romantic tour of the city as Allen has experienced it; like *Annie Hall* it is an essay on the difficulties of modern relationships, where commitment is a goal but one viewed with mixed emotions. Woody (here called Isaac or Ike) is a near-Woody, a prosperous but harassed television writer who is already down two marriages, his most recent ex (Meryl Streep) having gone off to live in a lesbian partnership.

For the moment the love of his life is a precocious seventeen-year-old (appealingly played by Mariel Hemingway). He cannot commit to her, he says, because he is too old (he is more than twice her age). Yet at seventeen she seems wiser than he is, his arguments an alibi for his fear of a permanent relationship. He takes up with Diane Keaton, an argumentative intellectual (cut from a quite different cloth than Annie Hall) on loan from his pal Michael Murphy. In one of Allen's most poignant endings, Woody/Ike sees too late that he really loved the Hemingway character but has now let her get away. In its way, *Manhattan*, with its mournful sense of the avoidable loss of love, is one of Allen's most touching films. Woody's alter egos are maturing emotionally, along with the filmmaker's ability to handle subtler and more testing material.

As evidence of the autonomy United Artists and his subsequent distributors have given him, Allen continues to shoot films in black and white where he finds it appropriate, in defiance of the industry's conventional (but probably correct) wisdom that young audiences in particular don't like to watch black-and-white films. *Manhattan* is almost impossible to conceive in color; it is a city (his city) of textures and shadows, the visual richness of an ornate past still readable in stone and in the images made by generations of photographers who shot in black and white. (World War II was fought in black and white, in newsreels and *Life* magazine, which is why feature films in color about the war lack the you-are-there bite of the others.)

Stardust Memories is also very nearly impossible to imagine in color. It is Woody's bitterly funny commentary on his own growing fame, more specifically on the fans who cried that he had no business abandoning comedy to do a dour psychological study like *Interiors*.

In execution, *Stardust Memories* becomes for Allen a further exploration of the possibilities of the movie medium. It recalls Fellini in several ways, including its gallery of unusual faces, rendered grotesque by the use of distorting lenses, extreme close-ups and low angles. Woody is Sandy Bates, a successful young filmmaker who has made a reputation for comedy but has now done a serious film and is being lionized at a weekend retrospective in a hotel on the Jersey shore. The film also recalls the Fellini of *8½* in Sandy's anxiety about what he will do next, and his fears not only of a creative drying-up but of mental collapse and madness with its lurid and frenzied imaginings.

Stardust Memories is a funny film; the fawning hangers-on are amusing in their pushy ways. But fame is seen as an isolating nightmare, a vision of being bitten to death by minnows. Yet within the high foolishness of the weekend's tribute, the film also continues the sequence of the protagonist's romances: his genuine love for Dorrie (Charlotte Rampling), who, however, is herself at the edge of madness and finally (seen in some more distorting close-ups as if being observed through the peep-hole of a padded cell) appears to have gone round the bend completely. There is the possibility of a new love with the beautiful Isobel (Marie-Christine Barrault from *Cousin Cousine*), but she cannot endure his distracted and divided attention and takes off with her children in tow. Daisy (Jessica Harper) reaches out to him as a kind of consolation prize. Yet at last Sandy is as solitary (in the midst of apparent plenty) as Ike was at the end of *Manhattan*, except that not one but two attractive partners have left him.

Seen on the rising graph of Allen's work, *Stardust Memories* displays a different, harder kind of humor, sardonic and rooted in observation rather more than in jokey comic invention. His handling of the fantasy elements—eerie moments on a commuter train—suggest further creative challenges conceived and conquered.

Amid the emotional and intellectual rigors of the previous films, *A Midsummer Night's Sex Comedy* (1982) is a beguiling change of pace—a benign, amusing, untroubling bucolic romp, with a tangle of relationships leading to a Feydeau-like sequence of concealments and narrow escapes, but played at a legato tempo as compared to the furious confusions of similar goings-on the young Woody wrote and participated in toward the end of *What's New, Pussycat? A Midsummer Night's Sex Comedy* is one of his airiest and most charming films, touched with magical elements and fine comic turns by Jose Ferrer and Allen himself as an endearingly nebbishy inventor.

Renoir once said that he had not made twenty-eight films but one film in twenty-eight versions or chapters. While there are significant themes that weave through Allen's films—increasingly evident as time passes—it is the quality of surprise that seems most characteristic of his work. The Woody persona—voluble, nervous, insecure, quick-witted, self-mocking—still runs through some of the films, most recently in *Manhattan Murder Mystery*. But more often each new film is in one way or another a startling departure from the last, as *Zelig* in 1983 was a departure from virtually everything that had gone before.

Zelig was a stunning cinematic challenge posed and met: to manipulate images, inserting Woody as Zelig into old newsreels and photographs, or into new photographs and newsreels cleverly degraded to look old, thus to establish the character of a man so desperate to be liked and accepted that he assumes chameleonlike the look and the attributes of those he is with. Not until *Forrest Gump* was anything of comparable cinematic ingenuity attempted on the same scale. Beyond the technical wizardry, of course, *Zelig* is an essay on insecurity, one of Woody's most frequent and visible concerns.

A particular kind of nostalgia, evoking the past with an affection that does not, however, remember that things were more wonderful than they were, is another of the recurring motifs in the films. *Broadway Danny Rose* in 1984, *The Purple Rose of Cairo* in 1985, and *Radio Days* in 1987 all reveal how wide the Allen variations on the theme of memory could be.

All three were, not least, star vehicles for Mia Farrow, who had first acted for Woody in *A Midsummer Night's Sex Comedy* and *Zelig*. *Broadway Danny Rose* is an affectionate tribute to the comedians and comedy writers who may still be schmoozing through the late-night hours in midtown delicatessens, exaggerating both their triumphs and disasters with audiences. In Danny, as one of the struggling small-time talent agents he knew in his early days, Woody created one of his most warmly sympathetic characters.

Mia's role as a hard-used, peroxide blonde gangster's moll was a stretch that she brought off with a fine gum-chewing flair. The action, centering on a madcap flight from thugs, is expertly executed and Nick Apollo Forte as a saloon singer with swollen pretensions is believably preposterous. The film, with its upbeat and sentimental ending, can be read as the work of a happy man.

The Purple Rose of Cairo is, by contrast, one of the most melancholy of Allen's creations once the laughter has died away. It is an examination of illusion and reality, with the films of the Depression seen as escapes (as they were) from all that was hard and defeating in life. Everything Woody had learned about the art of filmmaking—mastering the technical possibilities, generating characters of interest and depth, moving a story along, and, beyond all else, using film as a carrier of truth as the writer-director has discovered it—came together in this remarkable work. He had never before been quite so unyielding, nor so inventively funny.

The cinematic trickeries are breathtaking. Jeff Daniels in a pith helmet in a dreadful black-and-white movie walks off the screen and, in full color, into the audience. It's a brilliantly original idea; like the concept of *Zelig* it is a true astonishment, and the permutations are intricately worked out. With Daniels gone, the other characters on the screen are reduced to playing cards and griping. In the real world, Mia, married to a brute and stuck in a lousy waitressing job, seeks consolation at the movies and finds Jeff Daniels, who escorts her from her drab surroundings through the screen and into the black-and-white but glamorous film, where the now-amended plot continues with a swell evening in a nightclub. Daniels has less fun offscreen, wandering through Mia's grim town, where nobody abides by the rules of movie make-believe.

Woody plays out the complexity of illusion versus reality to the bitter end. The actor, as naive on screen as off, flies back to California with a wispy and fading sense of something meaningful having been discovered and lost. Mia, drowning in her terrible life, seeks comfort again in the darkness, this week in the romantic presence of Astaire and Rogers in full swing. It is one of Allen's best efforts, watchable again and again, and yielding new subtleties each time.

Radio Days is an unabashed celebration of the hold the medium had on the national imagination in the years before television. Woody himself is heard but not seen, his voice-over linking his skillful parodies of a wild variety of shows, from the agony hour of family counseling to quiz shows, the married couple chatting about their social life over breakfast to the late-afternoon adventure serials for kiddies (Wallace Shawn as "The Masked Avenger"), to the big bands and all the commercial jingles. A child actor plays the young Woody, lusting after a secret decoder pin, with dire consequences inflicted by parents and his rabbi. Mia is a seduced cigarette girl who ends as a radio gossip not unlike Louella O. Parsons. The film is a pleasing exercise of Allen's talents, lightly seasoned with those moments of burlesqued autobiography.

If *Interiors* looks at a family gravely dysfunctional and touched by tragedy, *Hannah and Her Sisters* (1986) examines in a quite different mode another family, resembling the first only in that the events center on the relations among three sisters. It is a colorful and complicated family which nevertheless remains functional whatever its temporary problems. The film became one of Allen's largest box-office successes: not surprising since it is also his warmest and most optimistic film. Its happy ending on the occasion of a Thanksgiving feast recalls Bergman's *Fanny and Alexander*, which had been released four years earlier.

It has one of his starriest casts. Michael Caine is Mia's husband, crazy with the hots for Barbara Hershey as her sister, who is married to an embittered artist played by Max von Sydow. Woody himself is co-starred, finding happiness at last with Dianne Wiest as the third sister. Lloyd Nolan and Maureen O'Sullivan (Mia's real mother) play the three girls' parents. They are troupers, well south of Lunt and Fontanne, who have had a theatrically stormy marriage but are now more or less contented, although still quick with needling remarks. The ending may be happy but there are patches of cloud. Adultery is played as farce, but its guilt and deceptions are hard felt, a marriage fails.

While the film undoubtedly reflects Woody's knowledge of Mia's own family, her sister, her mother, and the memories of her late and complicated father, the director John Farrow, the insights have as usual been thoroughly transmuted by the imagination. The legal notice can unblushingly say, "Any resemblence, etc." *Hannah and Her Sisters* suggests that the joke-teller has become a sure-handed storyteller, adept at sketching characters economically and moving a fairly webby plot briskly along.

After the *gemutlich* good cheer of *Hannah*, Allen returned to the cooler, sharper mode of *Interiors* to dissect a tangle of relationships in *September* (1987) and to chart the collapse of a delusive self-image in *Another Woman* in 1988. Both films convey a distance between the observer and the observed. Here the author-director seems more the objective witness than, as in other films, a man recollecting close personal experience, present or past. Yet both films have a fluidity and a distinctly cinematic flavor that *Interiors* in its theatrical austerity did not.

This seems true even though *September* is even more confined physically than *Interiors* was, taking place entirely within the walls of a Vermont country house (which could as well be a Chekhovian dacha) at a summer's end. Family and friends are at such cross-purposes as any Russian playwright could ask for. Mia plays an emotionally fragile woman who as a teenager killed the abusive gangster lover of her mother (Elaine Stritch, in an unforgettable, all-stops-out performance). She is still far from stable, forlornly in love with Sam Waterston as a summer beau who has just fallen for Mia's friend (Dianne Wiest), who in turn has just begun to realize she no longer loves her husband down in Philadelphia. The newly widowed next-door neighbor (Denholm Elliott) completes the mismatchings by being unrequitedly in love with Mia.

Mother and new husband (Jack Warden, colorful but not entirely convincing as a particle physicist) blow in for a visit, but the communication lines between mother and daughter are down and likely to stay that way. It's messy up there in Vermont, soap operatic but redeemed from soap opera by the tang of the dialogue and the dimensions of the characters. Warden proclaims the universe to be haphazard, morally neutral, unbelievably violent and likely to end as haphazardly as it began (a note of pessimism that can also be picked out as recurrent in the Allen *oeuvre*).

As in a play, people say what they think, and while there are close-ups, it is the dialogue that moves things along. If the film does not entirely escape the impression of proscenium theatricality, it achieves real emotional power as the characters struggle with their various anguishes.

Allen is a musician himself, and his use of music is always interesting and refreshing. In *September*, it is all "real," part of the scene rather than underscoring applied like cosmetics in the traditional way. An Art Tatum–Ben Webster album is heard on the stereo; Dianne Wiest as a garden-variety living room pianist plays standards whose titles are poignantly appropriate to the action ("I'm Confessin' That I Love You," "What'll I Do?").

Another Woman is an intense and engrossing study of the disintegration of a character, in a film that demonstrates again Woody's ability to evoke from his actors work of power and sensitivity. Gena Rowlands's portrait of an academic whose confident self-image collapses under the weight of a series of retroactive revelations of her self-centeredness has a soul-deep dramatic force.

The supporting performances are well etched: Ian Holm as her pompous, philandering husband, Gene Hackman as the good man she let get away (and who is obviously the better off for it). Mia Farrow has a relatively brief role as a woman confessing deep troubles to her psychiatrist, and overheard by Rowlands through a ventilating duct between the two suites. Blythe Danner and Sandy Dennis are excellent as other friends who in their ways erode the woman's confidences.

Another Woman gets out and about more than *Interiors* and *September*, but it remains essentially an almost claustrophobic character study, and a strong comment on the self-deception born of egoism and ambition. Allen, fifty-three when he made the film, had come a long way from the stand-up comic.

But he had not lost his acerbic sense of humor, and in reviewing his career, it is worth tipping one's hat to his short film "Oedipus Wrecks," with its inspired punning title. It was Allen's contribution to a three-segment film called *New York Stories* (1989). Martin Scorsese and Francis Ford Coppola did the other and less successful stories.

In little more than a half hour, Allen manages to exercise his gifts for absurdity and technical surprise, his interest in magic, his feeling for Manhattan, and his ongoing picture of the insecure son in the hands of an overpowering mother. Woody's tale of his mother disappearing during a magic trick and reappearing as a giant head in the sky hectoring her son's every move in a booming voice audible from Flatbush to Secaucus is exquisite nonsense. Mae Questel is terrific as Mama, Julie Kavner (an Allen regular) as a failed occultist, Mia as the fiancée who flees. Like everything Allen has done, the short is original, ingenious, and all Woody.

Crimes and Misdemeanors, which was also released in 1989, is another of Allen's masterworks, his most successful blending of comedy and high, philosophical seriousness. Woody and Mia head the cast, he as a documentary maker doing a piece on his fatuous brother-in-law, a television personality played by Alan Alda. But the figures who remain most potently in mind from the film are Martin Landau as the successful businessman who pays for the murder of his mistress—and gets away with it—and Angelica Huston as his victim. Jerry Orbach as Landau's brother, who arranges the hit out of reluctant fraternal loyalty, is another briefly seen but provocative presence, as is Sam Waterston as a rabbi who is going blind.

Woody, whose concerns with the great matters of love, death, guilt, and the existence or nonexistence of God have long since become more than items of graduate student comedy in his work, grapples most particularly in *Crimes and Misdemeanors* with the burden of guilt and the related question of the existence of God.

Allen's principal biographer, Eric Lax, describes him as a reluctant but pessimistic agnostic who would like to believe in God but cannot, quite. And although Woody jokes about the God question in *Love and*

Death, the handling is far more serious in *Crimes and Misdemeanors*. Human actions are seen to hinge on one's feelings about the existence of God. The Landau character is first racked with guilt about the death of his mistress, but when it is clear he is going to get away with the crime, it also becomes clear that life will go on, almost tranquilly. Presumably earthly guilt is manageable; punishment at the hands of a judging God would be a different matter—if there were a God. More than any of the films before it, *Crimes and Misdemeanors* successfully tests Allen's command of the language of film to express a writer's thoughts on themes that are subtle, relevant, timeless, and difficult.

Over the years Allen has created a succession of valentines (roles, at the very least) for the women in his life, commencing with Louise Lasser, then his wife, in *What's New, Pussycat?* and four subsequent films. Diane Keaton was first seen with him in *Play It Again, Sam*, which Allen wrote but Herbert Ross directed, and in six later films (so far), including *Annie Hall* most memorably, and *Manhattan Murder Mystery* in 1993. Mia Farrow appeared in thirteen Allen films, beginning with *A Midsummer Night's Sex Comedy* in 1982 and concluding with *Husbands and Wives* in 1992.

Alice (1990) was another gift to Mia, an opportunity to reveal more of her versatility as an actress. For Allen it was also a chance to comment on the vacuity of life among the underoccupied rich and the possibility of alternate life-choices.

Mia is the wife of a very rich businessman (William Hurt), living to shop and stay fit but increasingly aware of the shallowness of her life. A flirtation with Joe Mantegna as a parent at their children's school only underlines her unhappiness. With his talent for surprise, Woody creates a Chinese herb doctor (a lovely last performance by Keye Luke, remembered from the Charlie Chan films) who gives her various powers, including invisibility, the better to catch her husband in an infidelity. Another dosage makes her irresistible to all men, but the power (farcical in the working out) only convinces her more strongly than ever that she wants to be Mother Theresa, not the Vamp of Savannah.

It is a curious film, interesting in its originality and unpredictability, a sympathetic portrait of a woman trying to find herself. The set designs and the photography are sumptuous. *Alice* is neither as funny as the comedies nor as grueling as the harder psychological studies, but it is provocative in its quiet way, and it reveals again the range of Allen's imagination.

Just how wild that imagination can get was borne out quite amazingly by *Shadows and Fog* (1991), a dark, semifarcical homage to a certain style of early European cinema. As with *Zelig*, Allen seems to have set himself a five-finger exercise. Woody is a quavering wimp in a late-nineteenth-century village where a serial killer is at large, rival vigilante groups are forming, fog is continuous, and the lighting might have been provided by the Little Match Girl.

The setting is presumably Germany—the music on the soundtrack is from Kurt Weill. Anti-Semitism is an implicit theme in the film, which with all else is a parable on mob psychology and mob violence as ingredients of anti-Semitism.

The casting is both starry and somewhat against type. John Malkovich is a clown with a traveling, horse-drawn carnival. He lives with Mia but is having sport with Madonna, who lives with the carnival's strong man. Jodie Foster, Lily Tomlin, and Kathy Bates are ladies in the local brothel, the only well-lighted place in the village. Donald Pleasance is a semimad doctor who becomes one of the serialist's victims.

Even within Allen's widely divergent output, *Shadows and Fog* is a true curiosity, an extended and amusing *jeu d'esprit* but with a subtext as somber as you care to make it.

In 1991, at the urging of his longtime managers, Jack Rollins and Charles Joffe, Woody tried his hand at yet another aspect of creativity. Taking a small crew, including photographer Brian Hamill, to Rome, he wrote and directed five television commercials for an Italian chain of food stores called The Coop. In one, green alien creatures in their spaceship complain about the difficulty of finding good food on earth. A captive earthling begs for a ham sandwich from The Coop. In another, a man reminisces about the day in his childhood when his father, ignoring the sexy maid, caresses a shiny red apple—from The Coop, of course. What is beguiling is that even when dubbed by Italian actors, the commercials retain a distinctly transatlantic, Felliniesque flavor.

From so curious an endeavor Allen turned again to the kind of sharp-edged and bittersweet (or not so sweet) study of modern marriage he does with such insight. *Husbands and Wives* (1992) is startling, almost experimental in its cinematography. Carlo Di Palma's handheld camera does some sudden fast pans from one speaker to another early in the film that are hard and even dizzying to watch, but that heighten the film's jangly sense of relationships gone awry. There are also sudden, screen-filling close-ups of Mia, not repeated later with her or the other performers.

The principals speak to the camera, as to a psychiatrist who is taping the session, although there are also other glimpses of conversations with analysts. These punctuations are never explained, and in the film's sad and problematic last line, Woody asks the camera, "Is this over? Can I go?" The question is ambiguous. Is the session over? the taping for whatever documentary purpose? the analysis as a whole? or the film itself? (The film is certainly over; the end credits follow.) But the question is somehow also a reminder that we are watching a film, a fictional gloss on life, however mesmerized and moved we may have been. It is a device both Bergman and Jean-Luc Godard have used, as a way of suggesting, "Consider these matters in your own lives, not simply in the lives of these fictional characters." Used here, the question can be taken as a useful borrowing, or an implicit homage.

Woody is this time Jake Ross, a novelist who teaches writing at a college and is married to Mia, who works for an art magazine. Their friends Jack and Sally (Sydney Pollack and Judy Davis) precipitate the events of the story by announcing, with a show of cheerful confidence, that they are separating. Jack takes up with a sexy but witless aerobics instructor, Sally starts seeing one of Mia's fellow editors at the art magazine (Liam Neeson, the Schindler of *Schindler's List*). Woody as Jake falls in with a sexually omnivorous student, played with a kind of teasing calculation by Juliette Lewis.

Of all Allen's films about relationships, *Husbands and Wives* is the most painfully intimate, an essay on the terrifying tentativeness of relationships and on the difficulty in fully understanding another person, let alone one's self. And the ultimate lesson is that it takes accommodation to the point of willful self-deception to make marriages endure.

If the Pollack and Davis characters are reconciled at last, their cheerful confidence appears as shaky as it was at their separation. Mia and Neeson are married, but there is an edginess to their assurance that everything is just fine. Mia's first husband has called her a passive-aggressive personality who always gets her way in the end; the viewer suspects that Neeson doesn't totally disbelieve this, despite his protestations.

As for the Woody figure, he is, as he has been before, alone again, on temporary leave from the field of romance, having perceived at last that what he calls his taste for "kamikaze women" is destructive all the way around. His comments to the camera have an unmannered and melancholy directness that is a world away from the speed-talking neurotic of funnier days. His performance, and what might be called the resigned tenderness he projects, give *Husbands and Wives* a resonance unique among his social comedies.

Manhattan Murder Mystery, taking shape as it did amid the turmoil of Allen's private life gone public in 1993, seems in every sense an escapist film—an escapist entertainment for the audience and an avoidance of any kind of interpretation. It was a joyful screen reunion with the Diane Keaton of *Annie Hall* and a volubly funny entertainment that resolutely defies any attempt to find a message beyond "Have a good time," which is itself a perfectly adequate message.

Like *Shadows and Fog*, it is in its own way a five-finger exercise, Allen having fun with the mystery genre. Like Hitchcock's *Rear Window*, it is a murder mystery whose murder and whose mystery must at first be deduced from small clues. Woody's return to the quippy and tremulous neurotic of the earlier films and his rapid-fire cross talk with Keaton is entertaining (even if its relentless pace borders on the exhausting) and the plot is ingenious. Considered in the whole context of Allen's career, it qualifies as an interlude but, given the circumstances of its creation, it qualifies as well as a miracle of professionalism under private pressure.

There is nothing interludal about *Bullets Over Broadway* (1994), a sustained comic romp widely regarded as Allen's funniest work in years. Co-authored by Douglas McGrath, the film, about the producing of a play (an arena in which Woody has had considerable experience), is a beautifully designed and mounted farce with sharp observations about the posings and pretensions of actors and artists.

Not for the first time, Allen gathered a high-style ensemble for his film. John Cusack is the earnest, naive playwright just in from Pittsburgh with his idealism intact. Dianne Wiest's portrayal as the grandest of hard-drinking theatrical grande dames (with a mind like a steel trap) is gloriously flamboyant. Tracey Ullman as a giggly aging ingenue delivers some of the film's best jokes. Chazz Palminteri as a hoodlum with literary gifts, Jennifer Tilly as a gangster's moll, Joe Viterelli as the gangster, and Jim Broadbent as an actor with an overeating disorder are individually and collectively splendid.

Along with the fun Allen is taking aim at the artist as self-proclaimed genius. Rob Reiner is an unproduced playwright who explains that his work is too good to be seen, and he announces that "Every artist creates his own moral universe." Allen mocks a charge that has sometimes been leveled against artists, and he underscores the mockery by giving the words to a ridiculous figure in a nightshirt.

Just after finishing *Bullets Over Broadway*, Woody mentioned to his new producer, Jean Doumanian, that his first Broadway play, *Don't Drink the Water* (1966), would make a funny movie. (The play had been bought by Hollywood and filmed as a vehicle for Jackie Gleason in 1969, but Woody was not involved creatively.) Almost overnight Doumanian set a deal for Woody to write, direct, and star in *Don't Drink the Water* as his first-ever movie for television. It was broadcast on ABC in December 1994.

Woody and Julie Kavner are a Newark couple (he the first caterer to sculpt a bridegroom out of potato salad) who are forced to seek asylum in the American embassy in a fictional Iron Curtain country. Allen correctly saw no need to update a script whose broad characters and slapstick events are timeless. He assembled a bright supporting cast, including Michael J. Fox as the addled acting ambassador, newcomer Mayim Bialik as the couple's daughter, and Dom DeLuise as a priest who has been living in the embassy for six years and spends his time practicing magic tricks, few of which come off. It is a high-gloss and very funny work, with Woody marvelous as a kind of petulant senior nebbish.

As this book went to press, Allen was completing production on his newest film, *Mighty Aphrodite,* a further exploration of relationships, this time including parenthood. The film stars Allen, Helena Bonham Carter, and Mira Sorvino, and was shot in New York and on location in Taormina, Sicily.

What is remarkable is that Allen's career in film now covers thirty years and yet he is, in 1995, only sixty years old. Filmmakers as dissimilar as George Cukor and Luis Buñuel were making films into their eighties, and Hitchcock was preparing still another film when he was in his late seventies. In the next-to-last volume of their monumental *The Story of Civilization*, Will and Ariel Durant wrote that "barring lethal accident to the authors or to civilization," there would be a concluding volume, and so there was. Barring similar lethalities and given creative energy that has seemed inexhaustible, Woody Allen may even now be hardly more than halfway through his uniquely productive career. His place in film history is already high and secure, but it is probable that there are any number of surprises and triumphs yet to come. As Brian Hamill's photographs on the following pages make clear, Woody is still an *auteur* in motion, on both sides of the camera.

Overleaf: on location in the streets of New York for *Manhattan Murder Mystery* (1993). Woody Allen, with two longtime associates, Camera Operator Dick Mingalone and Dolly Grip Ronald "Red" Burke.

WOODY ALLEN
AT WORK

THE PHOTOGRAPHS
OF BRIAN
HAMILL

Woody as Alvy Singer, stand-up comic and man about town, in *Annie Hall* (1977).

Annie Hall. Several flashback scenes were filmed on location in the Coney Island section of Brooklyn, New York. Here, Woody utilizes a viewfinder to line up a shot.

Diane Keaton and Woody Allen in *Annie Hall*. One of Woody's own favorites, this breakthrough picture vaulted Keaton to stardom and even influenced fashion around the world.

A Midsummer Night's Sex Comedy (1982), a turn-of-the-century pastoral romantic comedy, was filmed in the summer of 1981 on the grounds of the Rockefeller Estate in Tarrytown, New York, and featured Woody and a pre-Raphaelite Mia Farrow at the very beginning of their extraordinary association.

On a beach in Southampton, Long Island, at "magic hour" (that brief interval when the sun is setting and the world is bathed in soft light), during the shooting of *Interiors* (1978). Woody confers with Gordon Willis, the most respected and influential American cinematographer of his generation, with whom he collaborated on eight consecutive films, from *Annie Hall* through *The Purple Rose of Cairo* (1985).

Manhattan (1979). Woody and co-star Mariel Hemingway rehearse a scene, a conversation in a café, while D.P. (Director of Photography) Gordon Willis views the action through the camera. The composition is a classic "over-the-shoulder" close-up—over Woody's right shoulder, featuring Hemingway. To Woody's right is a small lighting unit that serves as Hemingway's "eye light." The light is aimed, controlled, and diffused so as to give her eyes an attractive glow.

In a flashback "movie-within-the-movie" sequence in *Stardust Memories* (1980), Woody and co-star Charlotte Rampling kiss in the "rain," which is created by a special-effects crew using hoses and sprinklers placed just outside of frame on either side.

A Midsummer Night's Sex Comedy. Inside the house that was built
for the film on the Rockefeller Estate. While Woody goes over the
action with Julie Hagerty, Tony Roberts, also in the scene, looks on.
At left, Hair Stylist Romaine Greene, another longtime associate, does
a final touch-up.

Actress Charlotte Rampling, right, with Make-Up Artist Fern Buchner, another Woody Allen regular, during filming of *Stardust Memories*.

Marie-Christine Barrault in *Stardust Memories*.

With Production Designer Mel Bourne during filming of *Manhattan*. The production designer brings the director's vision to life through construction of sets; choice of locations, color schemes, set dressing, and props; and by working closely with the cinematographer and the costume designer. Along with Gordon Willis and Woody himself, Mel Bourne is chiefly responsible for the "look" of this and several other Woody Allen films.

During production of *Manhattan*. Woody in conversation with Script Supervisor Kay Chapin, who has worked steadily with him since *Annie Hall*. Chapin keeps track of all script revisions and modifications, works with the director and cinematographer to ensure that shots will "match" (join together in a logical way) in editing, and is responsible for continuity: all narrative and visual components of a scene must remain consistent from shot to shot.

In Central Park during filming of *Manhattan*. Woody keeps a hand on the camera, which has been secured to the back of an open-ended vehicle. A special wooden platform, complete with guardrail, has been devised and constructed by the grips, technicians responsible for, among numerous other things, the rigging of cameras and the safety of all crew. This arrangement—camera fixed to the back of a "camera car"—is used for "running shots," which capture action involving moving vehicles and dialogue scenes between characters in another car.

Stardust Memories. With Jessica Harper during a break in filming, at Planting Fields Arboretum on Long Island, New York. Behind, in the dark shirt, James Mazzola, Woody's Prop Master of many years, stands by with one of the several hot-air balloons later used in a breathtaking "magic hour" aerial sequence.

Woody in *Stardust Memories,* as a famous and popular filmmaker who is tormented by memories and fantasies, hounded by family, lovers, co-workers, and fans, and on the threshold of a nervous collapse.

Stardust Memories. Gordon Willis's photography and Mel Bourne's production design together evoke the artist's comically nightmarish world—bright and alienating, antiseptic and overwrought at the same time, and inhabited by strangers and hangers-on.

In *Annie Hall*, Woody questions the possibilities for happiness in love. Here, with two of the women in his life, played by Shelley Duvall and Carol Kane.

With then-newcomer Meryl Streep, in *Manhattan*.

On the set of *Interiors*, the first day of shooting. This set is the office of Woody's long-time manager Jack Rollins. Here Woody talks about a scene with his lead actress Diane Keaton.

Keaton in *Manhattan* and *Annie Hall*. Brian Hamill comments: "Diane is one of the nicest, and smartest, actresses in the movie business. She's so much more than just an actress—she has so many dimensions, serious interests in photography, art, and directing. In addition to being a fine actress and really sexy without trying to be, she's a real artist in her own right."

Interiors. To enhance the film's stark and ominous mood, Woody and Gordon Willis chose to shoot exteriors in the fall on an empty beach in Southampton, Long Island. Woody's preference for overcast days and rainy weather is illustrated here: sisters Kristin Griffith and Diane Keaton along the misty, windswept shore.

Interiors. Geraldine Page as Eve, the troubled family matriarch,
moments before she ends her own life by walking into the ocean.

Interiors. A flashback to happier times: sister Joey (Mary Beth Hurt) remembers her mother's dignity and beauty.

Diane Keaton as Renata and Mary Beth Hurt as Joey,
contemplative and angst-ridden sisters in *Interiors.*

Manhattan. Woody with Mariel Hemingway. Hamill remarks that cinematographer Gordon Willis is partial to silhouettes; in this film they are a prime visual motif. Hamill recalls that the rain on the apartment windows was a special effect, conjured up by Willis. "Woody loved the idea—Woody loves rain shots, which occur in many of his films. Clouds and rain are his kind of weather. For him, a nice day is a rainy day."

Manhattan. Woody and Diane in the sculpture garden of the Museum of Modern Art.

Stardust Memories. Left and overleaf: Again, the silhouette as visual motif. Inside, producers criticizing the filmmaker's work; outside, a surreal gathering of UFO followers.

Woody directs future star Sharon Stone in a brief early moment of
Stardust Memories. Opposite: The camera is perched on wooden
crates called "apple boxes" and stabilized with sandbags. Because of
the camera's straight-on position, a black material called "duvatine" has
been draped over it, so that it will not see itself reflected in the glass.

A *Midsummer Night's Sex Comedy*.
With Mary Steenburgen, Julie Hagerty
(partly hidden behind Woody), and
Tony Roberts. Hamill remembers, "My
daughter was a little baby then, and
there were lots of kids on the set, in the
middle of this incredibly bucolic location. It was a pleasure to come to work.
The main shooting areas were at the
house and by the brook in the woods.
Now both Woody and Gordon pre-
ferred to shoot in overcast weather—to
give a soft, even light to everything. So,
if we were at the brook and the sun
popped out, we'd hear, 'Okay, back to
the house! The sun's out! Back to the
house!' And we'd shoot in the house till
the sun went away again."

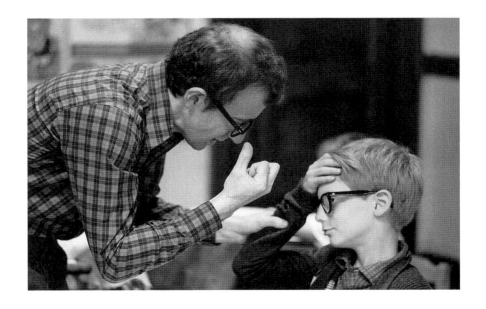

During filming of flashback scenes in *Annie Hall*. Here, Woody works with Jonathan Munk (his boyhood self) and a young actress named Brooke Shields.

Annie Hall. Growing up in Brooklyn: the Merry-Go-Round and Boardwalk at Coney Island.

With Gordon Willis during *Annie Hall*, *Manhattan*, and *Stardust Memories*: one of the central artistic collaborations in Woody's career, hence in American film of the last quarter century. Hamill says, "Woody would agree that if there's one person largely responsible for his visual education in this medium, that person is Gordon Willis."

New York City romance: *Manhattan* is regarded by many as the most magnificently photographed of all of Woody's films. Here, Woody and Diane Keaton extend their conversation into the wee hours in the imposing and gorgeous presence of the 59th Street Bridge. Photographed by Gordon Willis at 3:45 A.M., this composition, breathtaking at first viewing, remains the film's most indelible image.

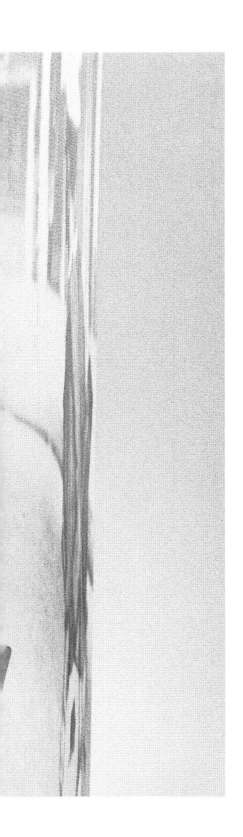

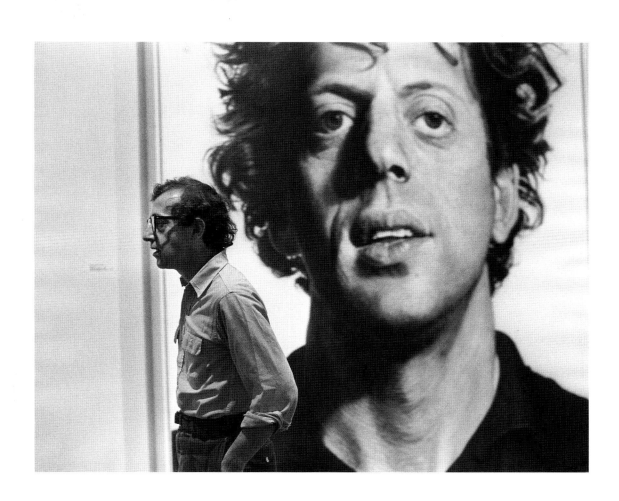

From *Stardust Memories* and *Manhattan*.

With his close friend, producer Jean Doumanian, who was
a frequent visitor to the set of *Manhattan*. Recently, Doumanian
was an executive producer of *Bullets Over Broadway* and *Don't
Drink the Water* (both 1994) and *Mighty Aphrodite* (1995).

Annie Hall. The ever-intense Christopher Walken, in one of
his earliest film roles, as Annie's somewhat disturbed brother.

The main cast of *A Midsummer Night's Sex Comedy*: left to right, Jose Ferrer, Tony Roberts, Woody Allen, Mia Farrow, Mary Steenburgen, and Julie Hagerty. As night falls, they gather around a magical device that enables them to see the happy spirits of past lovers frolicking in the forest.

A Midsummer Night's Sex Comedy: Paradise regained...but only for a moment. By the singing brook, in the middle of an enchanted night, Woody and Mia briefly recapture lost romance. From here, director and actress would make twelve more films together—in a row—a remarkable, unique partnership.

During production of *Annie Hall*.

As Leonard Zelig in *Zelig* (1983), Woody's brilliant mock-documentary about a mysterious, chameleonlike figure of the late 1920s and early 1930s, who keeps turning up different forms and identities, and becomes a media sensation and ultimately a hero.

Broadway Danny Rose (1984) is structured around a late-night conversation among a group of seasoned stand-up comics, who reminisce about an unforgettable talent manager named Danny Rose—played, of course, by Woody himself. Here, Woody directs the comedians at their table. These sequences were filmed on location inside New York's famous Carnegie Delicatessen on Seventh Avenue.

In *The Purple Rose of Cairo* (1985), Mia Farrow and Danny Aiello portray an unhappily married couple struggling to keep afloat during the Great Depression. Cecilia (Farrow) lives a life of poverty, anxiety, and profound drudgery. Her brutish husband (Aiello) adds to her misery by making domestic life intolerable. Her only pleasures come when she escapes to the local movie theater. There, one strange day, miraculously, a romantic character in the movie she is watching suddenly walks off the screen—and into her life, sending the narrative into a, myriad of fantastic, absurdly comical, and ultimately poignant twists and turns.

Shooting *Hannah and Her Sisters* (1986). A quintessential production configuration: Woody checks the composition through the camera; Dolly Grip "Red" Burke prepares to push the dolly forward; behind him an electrician waits on a ladder, ready to "tweak" a light; behind and to Woody's left, Camera Operator Dick Mingalone stands by (when it's time to roll, he, not Woody, will operate the camera); a camera assistant checks his focus control; and First Assistant Director Tom Reilly surveys the scene about to be shot, ready with his walkie-talkie to convey any additional directions from Woody to his cast and crew down the line.

Radio Days (1987). Woody orchestrates a scene on a partly neon-lit dance hall set.

Radio Days. Left to right: Woody, Director of Photography Carlo Di Palma, Camera Operator Dick Mingalone, and First Assistant Director Tom Reilly. During set-up and rehearsal of a shot, Woody instructs Reilly how he would like the scene to play; and Reilly, in turn, relays his directions through his walkie to his assistants and other crew members some distance away. This relationship—between director and first assistant—is central to the efficient operation of any film set.

Radio Days. With cinematographer Carlo Di Palma and First A.D. Tom Reilly. Here, Di Palma designs another moving shot. Says Hamill, "For Carlo, the camera *always* moves."

On East End Avenue in New York on the first day of shooting for *Hannah and Her Sisters*. Carlo Di Palma works out the first set-up of the day: the familiar Woody-Mia "walk and talk." This was Woody's first collaboration with Di Palma; to date, Di Palma has gone on to shoot eight more films with Woody.

The Purple Rose of Cairo. In this fantasy-comedy, Jeff Daniels (in pith helmet) portrays a movie character who, having fallen in love with Mia, asks her to stay with him—despite the fact that he is fictional. His fellow movie characters, stranded in the movie (the story can't proceed without him), look on anxiously.

The Purple Rose of Cairo. Mia Farrow in one of her best performances, as Cecilia, the unhappy and hapless housewife.

The Purple Rose of Cairo. Danny Aiello as Monk, the mean, possessive, and irresponsible husband.

Mia Farrow in *The Purple Rose of Cairo*. Production Designer Stuart Wurtzel's dark, somber color scheme underscores the tedium and drabness of this character's life—a life uplifted and redeemed in part by the movies.

Mia Farrow in *Zelig*. On the following pages, a gallery of portraits.

From *Hannah and Her Sisters*.

From *Broadway Danny Rose*.

From *The Purple Rose of Cairo.*

Woody directs his three lead actresses in *Hannah and Her Sisters*. Much of this film was shot inside Mia Farrow's apartment overlooking Central Park in New York.

From *Hannah and Her Sisters*. Dianne Wiest and Woody as unexpected mates, in the film's finale.

Hannah and Her Sisters. Mia, as oldest
sister Hannah, with Barbara Hershey, as
younger sister Lee. A typical composition
from this film, graphically linking these
two characters, whose lives encircle one
another and intertwine.

Hannah and Her Sisters. Woody
directs Barbara Hershey and the great
Swedish actor Max von Sydow, whom
Woody had long admired for his work
in Ingmar Bergman's films.

On a street in SoHo, New York City, during filming of *Hannah and Her Sisters*. Woody and Michael Caine "block" the shot (choreograph and rehearse the actors' positions and movements and the timing of their lines).

Broadway Danny Rose. Mia as Tina Vitale, a mobster's moll—brash, brassy, and tough. Woody wrote this role so that she could play a harder, nastier character. Mia has commented that she deliberately kept her sunglasses on in much of the film as another way of projecting that toughness.

The classroom is a motif in Woody's films. Here, an affectionate
remembrance from the nostalgic *Radio Days*: two variations on
"Show and Tell."

*R*adio Days. Above: Near the boardwalk in Far Rockaway, Woody prepares a scene with his young self Seth Green (in the red shirt) and his neighborhood buddies. At left is First A.D. Tom Reilly, who, according to Hamill, "is never more than a few feet away from Woody." At far left is cinematographer Carlo Di Palma.

*R*ight: A family portrait. Left to right, Julie Kavner, Seth Green, and Michael Tucker, during filming of a scene in Brooklyn's Prospect Park. Hamill recounts, "We've shot here many times over the years, and whenever we do, Woody and I always reminisce about growing up in Brooklyn. We didn't know each other then, but for both of us, this park is an old stamping ground."

*F*ar right: One of Woody's own favorites, *Radio Days* is an anthology of reminiscences of growing up in Brooklyn in the turbulent 1940s. It has been acclaimed for its wonderfully nostalgic score, spectacular period re-creation, and dazzling production and costume design. Cinematography by Carlo Di Palma; production design by Santo Loquasto; costume design by Jeffrey Kurland.

Rehearsing the scenes at the comics' table for *Broadway Danny Rose*. Seated against the wall is Woody's father, Martin Konigsberg, known affectionately to all as "Mr. K."

On the set of *Hannah and Her Sisters*. In the film, Mia Farrow and Barbara Hershey (behind, with Woody) portray two sisters; their parents are played by Lloyd Nolan (left) and Mia's real-life mother, Maureen O'Sullivan (right).

The Purple Rose of Cairo. One of Woody's favorite actresses, the radiant Dianne Wiest. A white tape-mark on the sofa (bottom left) indicates the exact position she must assume during the shot.

Danny Aiello, as a sentimental hood with friends in high places, in *Radio Days*.

Hannah and Her Sisters. The three sisters: Mia Farrow, Barbara Hershey, and Dianne Wiest.

Mia and sister Stephanie, as waitresses in a diner, in *The Purple Rose of Cairo*.

Jeff Daniels and Glenne Headley in the bordello, in *The Purple Rose of Cairo*.

On the set of *Zelig*. Expert equestriennes Mia and Stephanie Farrow.

On the set of *The Purple Rose of Cairo.*

Radio Days. During a break in filming, Woody visits with Mia and infant Dylan (asleep on the sofa).

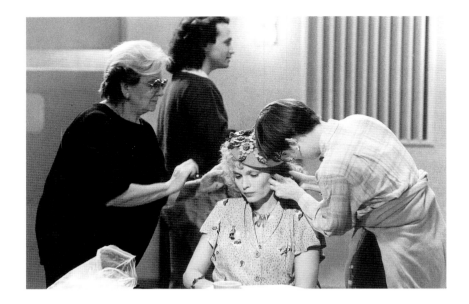

On the set of *Radio Days*: moments before shooting, Hair Stylist Romaine Greene (left) and Women's Wardrobe Supervisor Patricia Eiben (right) take their "last looks" (perform their final touch-ups on an actor's costume, hair, and make-up). Behind them: Costume Designer Jeffrey Kurland.

On the set of *Broadway Danny Rose*, Woody is attended to by his perennial Hair and Make-Up Department: left, Romaine Greene (Hair Stylist) and, right, Fern Buchner (Make-Up Artist)—known, affectionately, to the crew as "the Salad Sisters."

Woody and Mia in *Broadway Danny Rose*.

September (1987). This ensemble "chamber" drama about a revelatory weekend at a country house in Vermont marked the seventh collaboration between Woody Allen and Mia Farrow.

September. Though set in and around a country house in rural Vermont, this film was shot entirely on sets built on a sound stage at Kaufman Astoria Studios in Queens, New York. The effect of a sunlit interior is created by powerful lights positioned outside the windows.

Crimes and Misdemeanors (1989). At a night exterior location with veteran New York actor Jerry Orbach.

Shadows and Fog (1991). This film, too, was shot on constructed sets at Kaufman Astoria Studios. Here, on the bordello set, Woody prepares a complicated shot—a 360-degree pan (the camera slowly rotates one full circle), which catches pieces of dialogue spoken in turn by several actors. Behind, paying close attention, are Lily Tomlin and Mia Farrow.

Alice (1990). With Judy Davis and Joe Mantegna.

With the great Swedish cinematographer Sven Nykvist, on the set of *Another Woman* (1988). On every film he has made since *Annie Hall*, Woody has collaborated with one of three of the greatest cinematographers in film history: Nykvist, Gordon Willis, and Carlo Di Palma.

A humorous pause on the bordello set of *Shadows and Fog*. The camera is in position, ready for its 360-degree spin; and, left to right, Jodie Foster, Lily Tomlin, and Mia Farrow stand by.

Alice. Woody "makes an adjustment" in a scene with Joe Mantegna...

...and Mantegna performs as directed.

Crimes and Misdemeanors. Alan Alda as an opportunistic, womanizing, and monumentally egotistical television director. Here, in a conveniently deserted conference room, he works his "magic" on a new friend. Moody cinematography by Sven Nykvist. Production design by Santo Loquasto.

On the set of *Shadows and Fog,* with John Cusack.

Lining up a shot for *Shadows and Fog.* Woody handholds the camera
to help determine the best angle and composition. D.P. Carlo Di Palma
(center, next to the column) looks on; and First A.D. Tom Reilly stands
to his right. Featured in the shot are Jodie Foster and Kathy Bates.

Shadows and Fog. Anne Lange, Jodie Foster,
and Kathy Bates as "working girls."

Another Woman. Gena Rowlands as Marion, a scholar and writer who, one day, pauses to reevaluate her life and herself.

Another Woman. The illustrious John Houseman in his last role, as the stern and stubborn patriarch of Marion's family.

Alice. Mia Farrow portrays a woman in turmoil whose friends persuade her to see an acupuncturist named Dr. Yang, played by Keye Luke. Dr. Yang turns out to have a few other skills, including some magical ones. In the course of the story, with his help, Alice becomes invisible, learns to fly, even brings a dead lover back to life. Here, Woody rehearses a scene in which Dr. Yang hypnotizes Alice.

Alice. Woody and cinematographer Carlo Di Palma wait out the rain outside the Central Park Zoo on the first day of shooting.

Alice. The excellent character actor Keye Luke, as the wizard-like Dr. Yang. Woody had long wanted to work with him (he is perhaps best remembered as Charlie Chan's "Number One Son"). This was his farewell performance; he died shortly after filming was completed.

Crimes and Misdemeanors. One side of this highly praised and much debated bipartite film concerns a respectable married man (Martin Landau) who grows desperate to end an increasingly untenable adulterous relationship. Here, Landau with Angelica Huston: the lovers in better times.

Angelica Huston, distraught, frantic, obsessed, in *Crimes and Misdemeanors*. Woody considers her a genius.

Woody and Carlo, on the set of *Shadows and Fog*.

On the street during filming of *Alice*. The basic set-up for the traditional "walk and talk" shot: At far right, Mia Farrow and Joe Mantegna speak their lines while walking. The camera is fixed to the dolly, a movable platform large enough also to seat the camera operator (Dick Mingalone) and an assistant (Mike Green). Also secured to the platform is a light fixture (with diffusion material placed in front of it to soften the light). A dolly grip pushes the entire "rig," gently, steadily, smoothly, over a long section of track. The camera thus "tracks" alongside the walking actors at their pace. Bright orange traffic cones mark off the work area, providing a measure of safety against cars passing by between takes. Director of Photography Carlo Di Palma, in the long coat, oversees the rehearsal.

Alec Baldwin as Mia Farrow's resurrected lover, in *Alice*.

Alice. In one of several fantasy sequences, Alice (played by Mia Farrow) is momentarily reunited with an old lover who has died (played by Alec Baldwin). In this scene, they fly. To create the illusion, Woody and Carlo utilize a special-effects process called "blue screen." In a studio, the actors are suspended in midair and photographed in flying poses against the blue screen. Exterior backgrounds are photographed separately. Later, in a film lab, the disparate elements are joined to form a composite image of the characters in flight.

With Gena Rowlands and Gene Hackman in Manhattan's Riverside Park, during filming of *Another Woman*. The story concerns Marion (Rowlands), an emotionally guarded woman who chooses suddenly to confront memories and feelings she has long suppressed. The narrative structure is complex, involving daydreams, fantasies, and memories, all woven seamlessly into the real-time fabric of the film. Here, Woody and his actors prepare for a scene in which Marion recollects—and, at last, accepts—the passionate love once offered her by an ardent suitor, played by Hackman.

Discussing a scene with Blythe Danner, on the set of *Another Woman*.

Another Woman. With Gena Rowlands and Philip Bosco. In this scene, also a flashback, Marion confronts her lover (Bosco) about her abortion, and must hold her ground against his angry accusations of selfishness. The scene begins as a memory—we see the young Marion (standing behind). But the memory is so powerful and immediate that she enters it; and the present-day Marion carries the confrontation to its close.

Another Woman. Martha Plimpton and Josh Hamilton as young lovers. Plimpton plays Gena Rowlands's affectionate and caring but critical step-daughter. In this scene, imagined by Rowlands, Plimpton offers a candid assessment of her stepmother's character.

Crimes and Misdemeanors. Arguably Woody's most complex achievement to date, this multilayered film tells two very different kinds of stories simultaneously, and neatly joins them only at the end. In one story, Woody is an idealistic documentary filmmaker who, when he is not pursuing a producer (played by Mia Farrow), gives his niece an education in the cinema by taking her to matinees on Bleecker Street. Above: with the niece, played by Jenny Nichols (whose father is Mike). Opposite: with Mia, showing her footage from his documentary about an aging philosopher.

Woody and Mia, on the set of *Shadows and Fog*.

Shadows and Fog. With its bohemian characters, darkness and shadows, sinister, fog-shrouded streets, and Kafkaesque, nightmarish mood, this film is one of Woody's most visually arresting. Here, he works with John Malkovich and Mia Farrow.

Shadows and Fog. Malkovich and Farrow find their way in the dark.

Madonna and circus strong-
man Dennis Vestunis, on the
set of *Shadows and Fog*.
Below: Woody directs, as
Madonna looks on.

Michael Kirby as a killer on the loose, in *Shadows and Fog*.

Woody and Mia in the middle of an expressionist cityscape, in *Shadows and Fog*.

Manhattan Murder Mystery. On location in New York City's East Village. Woody listens to a rehearsal of one of the closing scenes from the film, a dialogue between Alan Alda and Angelica Huston as they exit a police station and saunter down the street. At left, First A.D. Tom Reilly. In the background, by their cart, the Sound Department: Sound Recordist James Sabat and his brother, Boom Operator Louis Sabat.

In Tribeca in downtown New York City, with Judy Davis, during filming of *Husbands and Wives* (1992). The sky is overcast, providing an unchanging, soft, even light—Woody's favorite light for exterior shooting.

Don't Drink the Water (1994). Woody with Mayim Bialik and Michael J. Fox, in a made-for-television adaptation of his 1966 play about a vacationing New Jersey family mistaken for spies in an unnamed Iron Curtain country. A 1969 film version starred Jackie Gleason and Estelle Parsons; Woody had never seen it until he began work on this project.

Bullets Over Broadway (1994). Dianne Wiest, as Helen Sinclair, a bombastic, over-the-hill, and comically vain grande dame of the theater. Here, she remembers— and re-enacts—moments from her "glorious" past.

At work on one of five television commercials for an Italian food-store chain called The Coop. At right, cinematographer Carlo Di Palma, First Assistant Director Tom Reilly, and Script Supervisor Kay Chapin. At left, a team of prop and special-effects technicians fit actors into their "pod" costumes. The actors portray aliens who are upset about the difficulty of locating good food on earth. In the middle of it all, Woody, with what Hamill describes as "his distinctive New York walk."

During production of another of the commercials, Woody demonstrates how to make love to an apple.

The always serious yet animated Carlo Di Palma, setting up a shot for one of the commercials. These exteriors were filmed outside Rome in the summer of 1991.

Liam Neeson and Judy Davis, in *Husbands and Wives*.

With Juliette Lewis in Riverside Park, during filming
of *Husbands and Wives*.

Juliette Lewis, in *Husbands and Wives*.

With Diane Keaton in Central Park during filming of *Manhattan Murder Mystery.* In this scene, later dropped from the picture, Woody expresses his love for this spot.

Manhattan Murder Mystery. Woody and Diane Keaton portray a couple with decidedly different views about a possible murderer in their midst. Keaton, whose life lacks excitement, is thrilled and energized by her pursuit and her amateur detective work; Woody, on the other hand, is reluctant—comically so—to become involved. This film united Woody and Diane for the first time since *Radio Days* (1987).

On the set of *Manhattan Murder Mystery*. Woody and Carlo exchange opinions about the design of the next shot.

Bullets Over Broadway. In Central Park, Woody talks with his lead actor, John Cusack, who portrays a struggling, idealistic playwright. Cusack had worked earlier with Woody, in *Shadows and Fog.*

With Dianne Wiest on the set of *Bullets Over Broadway.*

Bullets Over Broadway. Chazz Palminteri as an artistic gangster named Cheech, and Debi Mazur as a flapper.

Bullets Over Broadway. A spectacular Prohibition Era nightclub called The Three Deuces was re-created in a ballroom inside the old New Yorker Hotel on the West Side of New York City. (This location was also used to construct the Depression Era nightclub in *Radio Days.*) Production design by Santo Loquasto. Costume design by Jeffrey Kurland.

Bullets Over Broadway. John Cusack and Chazz Palminteri
on a street in Brooklyn Heights.

Bullets Over Broadway. Woody directs Jennifer Tilly,
a mobster's no-talent girlfriend.

On the set of *Bullets Over Broadway*, Woody demonstrates how he would like the action to be performed in a particularly farcical scene...

...and here we see the results. In the scene, a gangster's girlfriend (Jennifer Tilly), dallying with a new lover (Jim Broadbent), is interrupted when her boyfriend pays a surprise visit. While she holds him off, her lover attempts a hasty exit—out the window.

Tracey Ullman and Dianne Wiest
in *Bullets Over Broadway.*

John Cusack and Mary-Louise Parker, a harried playwright and his tolerant wife, in *Bullets Over Broadway*.

Directing Edward Herrmann and Michael J. Fox in *Don't Drink the Water.*

With Julie Kavner, in *Don't Drink the Water.*

Michael J. Fox, as a diplomat's son, in *Don't Drink the Water.*

On location in Tarrytown, New York, during production of
Mighty Aphrodite (1995). Woody confers with Costume
Designer Jeffrey Kurland and First Assistant Director Tom Reilly.
Behind them, the technical crew sets up.

Mira Sorvino and Michael Rapaport in a scene from *Mighty Aphrodite*.

F. Murray Abraham as the leader of a Greek chorus in *Mighty Aphrodite*. These scenes were shot on location in Taormina, Sicily.

Left: *Mighty Aphrodite*. David Ogden Stiers (center stage), Olympia Dukakis (standing on the first step), and (far right) Woody's perennial Costume Designer Jeffrey Kurland.

Woody with his crew in Taormina. Behind and to his right,
cinematographer Carlo Di Palma.

Mighty Aphrodite. With Helena Bonham Carter and Peter Weller.

With Carlo Di Palma, during filming of *Husbands and Wives*.

With fellow director-actor Sydney Pollack, on the set of
Husbands and Wives.

Under the boardwalk in Far Rockaway during production of *Radio Days*.

Manhattan Murder Mystery. The mirror mirrored: In the final sequence, Woody comes to Keaton's rescue in an old movie house that is running Orson Welles's 1948 classic *The Lady from Shanghai*. The theater is badly in need of renovation; there are mirrors and large freestanding windows everywhere. We see, reflected, the famous climactic "Hall of Mirrors" shoot-out from Welles's film, while Woody's own pursuit culminates in similarly bewildering fashion.

Near the conclusion of *Hannah and Her Sisters*, a profoundly uncertain Woody enters the old Metro theater on upper Broadway, where, in the presence of the Marx Brothers, he has a revelation. Film as education, inspiration, and redemption—a familiar theme in Woody's work.

Shadowboxing with Danny Aiello, during production of *The Purple Rose of Cairo*. Camera Operator Dick Mingalone referees this match between Brooklyn and the Bronx (where Aiello grew up).

During production of *Annie Hall*.

With Brian Hamill's daughter, Cara.

With daughter Dylan, on the set of "Oedipus Wrecks," Woody's contribution to *New York Stories* (1989).

Lighter moments during production of *Broadway Danny Rose* and *Shadows and Fog*.

Shadowed by Death, on a beach in Southampton, during production of *Interiors*.

During filming of "Oedipus Wrecks": Woody in his domain, his beloved Manhattan.

Left and above, Woody working on *Annie Hall*.

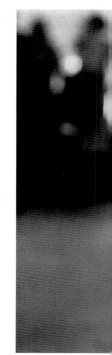

During filming of *Manhattan*. Brian Hamill on Woody Allen: "Woody's a very unpretentious, feet-on-the-ground artist, who never wears his intelligence like a badge on his sleeve. Rather, he simply uses his work to help him though the struggle of life. All of us who have had the privilege of working with him have come away artistically rewarded; and, personally, I feel that I've also received from him an unexpected gift of loyalty, spilled over from the workplace into friendship."

FILMOGRAPHY

Annie Hall (1977)
A Jack Rollins–Charles H. Joffe Production
Associate Producer: Fred T. Gallo
Editor: Ralph Rosenblum, A.C.E.
Art Director: Mel Bourne
Costume Designer: Ruth Morley
Director of Photography: Gordon Willis, A.S.C.
Executive Producer: Robert Greenhut
Producer: Charles H. Joffe
Writers: Woody Allen and Marshall Brickman
Director: Woody Allen
Cast: Woody Allen, Colleen Dewhurst, Shelley Duvall, Carol Kane, Diane Keaton, Janet Margolin, Tony Roberts, Paul Simon, Christopher Walken
A United Artists Release. Color. 93 minutes

Interiors (1978)
A Jack Rollins–Charles H. Joffe Production
Casting: Juliet Taylor
Editor: Ralph Rosenblum, A.C.E.
Production Designer: Mel Bourne
Costume Designer: Joel Schumacher
Director of Photography: Gordon Willis, A.S.C.
Executive Producer: Robert Greenhut
Producer: Charles H. Joffe
Writer and director: Woody Allen
Cast: Kristin Griffith, Mary Beth Hurt, Richard Jordan, Diane Keaton, E.G. Marshall, Geraldine Page, Maureen Stapleton, Sam Waterston
A United Artists Release. Color. 83 minutes

Manhattan (1979)
A Jack Rollins–Charles H. Joffe Production
Casting: Juliet Taylor
Music: George Gershwin
Editor: Susan E. Morse, A.C.E.
Production Designer: Mel Bourne
Costume Designer: Albert Wolsky
Director of Photography: Gordon Willis, A.S.C.
Executive Producer: Robert Greenhut
Producer: Charles H. Joffe
Writers: Woody Allen and Marshall Brickman

Director: Woody Allen
Cast: Woody Allen, Anne Byrne, Mariel Hemingway, Diane Keaton, Michael Murphy, Meryl Streep
A United Artists Release. Black and white. 96 minutes

Stardust Memories (1980)
A Jack Rollins–Charles H. Joffe Production
Casting: Juliet Taylor
Editor: Susan E. Morse, A.C.E.
Production Designer: Mel Bourne
Costume Designer: Santo Loquasto
Director of Photography: Gordon Willis, A.S.C.
Executive Producers: Jack Rollins, Charles H. Joffe
Producer: Robert Greenhut
Writer and director: Woody Allen
Cast: Woody Allen, Marie-Christine Barrault, Jessica Harper, Charlotte Rampling, Tony Roberts
A United Artists Release. Black and white. 89 minutes

A Mid-Summer Night's Sex Comedy (1982)
A Jack Rollins–Charles H. Joffe Production
Associate Producer: Michael Peyser
First Assistant Director: Fredric B. Blankfein
Second Assistant Directors: Thomas Reilly, Anthony Gittelson
Casting: Juliet Taylor
Music: Felix Mendelssohn
Editor: Susan E. Morse, A.C.E.
Production Designer: Mel Bourne
Costume Designer: Santo Loquasto
Director of Photography: Gordon Willis, A.S.C.
Executive Producer: Charles H. Joffe
Producer: Robert Greenhut
Writer and director: Woody Allen
Cast: Woody Allen, Mia Farrow, Jose Ferrer, Julie Haggerty, Tony Roberts, Mary Steenburgen
An Orion Pictures Release. Color. 87 minutes

Zelig (1983)
A Jack Rollins–Charles H. Joffe Production
Associate Producer: Michael Peyser

Casting: Juliet Taylor
Music: composed and adapted by Dick Hyman
Creative Coordinator: Gail Sicilia
Editor: Susan E. Morse, A.C.E.
Production Designer: Mel Bourne
Costume Designer: Santo Loquasto
Director of Photography: Gordon Willis, A.S.C.
Executive Producer: Charles H. Joffe
Producer: Robert Greenhut
Writer and director: Woody Allen
Narrator: Patrick Horgan
Cast: Woody Allen, Garrett Brown, Mia Farrow, Stephanie Farrow, Will Holt, Sol
	Lomita, John Rothman, Deborah Rush, Marianne Tatum, Mary Louise Wilson
An Orion Pictures Release. Black and white. 79 minutes

Broadway Danny Rose (1984)

A Jack Rollins–Charles H. Joffe Production
Editor: Susan E. Morse, A.C.E.
Production Designer: Mel Bourne
Costume Designer: Jeffrey Kurland
Director of Photography: Gordon Willis, A.S.C.
Executive Producer: Charles H. Joffe
Producer: Robert Greenhut
Writer and director: Woody Allen
Cast: Woody Allen, Sandy Baron, Milton Berle, Mia Farrow, Nick Apollo Forte,
	Jackie Gayle, Morty Gunty, Will Jordan, Corbett Monica, Jack Rollins,
	Howard Storm
An Orion Pictures Release. Black and white. 85 minutes

The Purple Rose of Cairo (1985)

A Jack Rollins–Charles H. Joffe Production
Associate Producers: Michael Peyser, Gail Sicilia
Casting: Juliet Taylor
Original music: Dick Hyman
Editor: Susan E. Morse, A.C.E.
Production Designer: Stuart Wurtzel
Costume Designer: Jeffrey Kurland
Director of Photography: Gordon Willis, A.S.C.
Executive Producer: Charles H. Joffe
Producer: Robert Greenhut
Writer and director: Woody Allen
Cast: Danny Aiello, Karen Akers, Zoe Caldwell, Alexander H. Cohen, Jeff Daniels,
	Juliana Donald, Annie Joe Edwards, Mia Farrow, Stephanie Farrow, Edward
	Herrmann, Van Johnson, Peter McRobbie, Irving Metzman, Milo O'Shea,
	John Rothman, Deborah Rush, Camille Saviola, Michael Tucker, Dianne
	Wiest, John Wood
An Orion Pictures Release. Color and black and white. 82 minutes

Hannah and Her Sisters (1986)

A Jack Rollins–Charles H. Joffe Production
Casting: Juliet Taylor
Editor: Susan E. Morse, A.C.E.
Production Designer: Stuart Wurtzel
Costume Designer: Jeffrey Kurland
Director of Photography: Carlo Di Palma, A.I.C.
Executive Producers: Jack Rollins, Charles H. Joffe
Producer: Robert Greenhut
Writer and director: Woody Allen
Cast: Woody Allen, Michael Caine, Mia Farrow, Carrie Fisher, Barbara Hershey,
	Lloyd Nolan, Maureen O'Sullivan, Daniel Stern, Max von Sydow, Dianne Wiest
An Orion Pictures Release. Color. 106 minutes

Radio Days (1987)

A Jack Rollins–Charles H. Joffe Production
Associate Producers: Ezra Swerdlow, Gail Sicilia
Casting: Juliet Taylor
Musical supervision: Dick Hyman
Editor: Susan E. Morse, A.C.E.
Production Designer: Santo Loquasto
Costume Designer: Jeffrey Kurland
Director of Photography: Carlo Di Palma, A.I.C.
Executive Producers: Jack Rollins, Charles H. Joffe
Producer: Robert Greenhut
Writer and director: Woody Allen
Cast: Danny Aiello, Jeff Daniels, Mia Farrow, Seth Green, Robert Joy, Julie Kavner,
	Diane Keaton, Julie Kurnitz, Renee Lippin, Kenneth Mars, Josh Mostel, Tony
	Roberts, Wallace Shawn, Michael Tucker, David Warrilow, Dianne Wiest
An Orion Pictures Release. Color. 89 minutes

September (1987)

A Jack Rollins–Charles H. Joffe Production
Casting: Juliet Taylor
Editor: Susan E. Morse, A.C.E.
Production Designer: Santo Loquasto
Costume Designer: Jeffrey Kurland
Director of Photography: Carlo Di Palma, A.I.C.
Executive Producers: Jack Rollins, Charles H. Joffe
Producer: Robert Greenhut
Writer and director: Woody Allen
Cast: Jane Cecil, Denholm Elliott, Mia Farrow, Rosemary Murphy, Elaine Stritch,
	Jack Warden, Sam Waterston, Ira Wheeler, Dianne Wiest
An Orion Pictures Release. Color. 82 minutes

Another Woman (1988)

A Jack Rollins–Charles H. Joffe Production

Casting: Juliet Taylor
Editor: Susan E. Morse, A.C.E.
Production Designer: Santo Loquasto
Costume Designer: Jeffrey Kurland
Director of Photography: Sven Nykvist, A.S.C.
Executive Producers: Jack Rollins, Charles H. Joffe
Produced by: Robert Greenhut
Writer and director: Woody Allen
Cast: Philip Bosco, Betty Buckley, Blythe Danner, Sandy Dennis, Mia Farrow, Gene Hackman, Josh Hamilton, Ian Holm, Martha Plimpton, Gena Rowlands, David Ogden Stiers, Harris Yulin
An Orion Pictures Release. Color. 84 minutes

"Oedipus Wrecks" in **New York Stories** (1989)
A Jack Rollins–Charles H. Joffe Production
Casting: Juliet Taylor
Editor: Susan E. Morse, A.C.E.
Production Designer: Santo Loquasto
Costume Designer: Jeffrey Kurland
Director of Photography: Sven Nykvist, A.S.C.
Executive Producers: Jack Rollins, Charles H. Joffe
Producer: Robert Greenhut
Writer and director: Woody Allen
Cast: Woody Allen, Mia Farrow, Julie Kavner, Mae Questel
A Touchstone Pictures Release. Color. 39 minutes

Crimes and Misdemeanors (1989)
A Jack Rollins–Charles H. Joffe Production
Casting: Juliet Taylor
Editor: Susan E. Morse, A.C.E.
Production Designer: Santo Loquasto
Costume Designer: Jeffrey Kurland
Director of Photography: Sven Nykvist, A.S.C.
Executive Producers: Jack Rollins, Charles H. Joffe
Producer: Robert Greenhut
Writer and director: Woody Allen
Cast: Caroline Aaron, Alan Alda, Woody Allen, Claire Bloom, Mia Farrow, Joanna Gleason, Angelica Huston, Martin Landau, Jenny Nichols, Jerry Orbach, Stephanie Roth, Sam Waterston, Grace Zimmerman
An Orion Pictures Release. Color. 104 minutes

Alice (1990)
A Jack Rollins–Charles H. Joffe Production
Associate Producers: Thomas Reilly, Jane Read Martin
Casting: Juliet Taylor
Co-Producers: Helen Robin, Joseph Hartwick
Editor: Susan E. Morse, A.C.E.

Production Designer: Santo Loquasto
Costume Designer: Jeffrey Kurland
Director of Photography: Carlo Di Palma, A.I.C.
Executive Producers: Jack Rollins, Charles H. Joffe
Producer: Robert Greenhut
Writer and director: Woody Allen
Cast: Alec Baldwin, Blythe Danner, Judy Davis, Mia Farrow, William Hurt, Keye Luke, Joe Mantegna, Bernadette Peters, Cybill Shepherd, Gwen Verdon
An Orion Pictures Release. Color. 106 minutes

Shadows and Fog (1991)
A Jack Rollins–Charles H. Joffe Production
Associate Producer: Thomas Reilly
Casting: Juliet Taylor
Co-Producers: Helen Robin, Joseph Hartwick
Editor: Susan E. Morse, A.C.E.
Production Designer: Santo Loquasto
Costume Designer: Jeffrey Kurland
Director of Photography: Carlo Di Palma, A.I.C.
Executive Producers: Jack Rollins, Charles H. Joffe
Producer: Robert Greenhut
Writer and director: Woody Allen
Cast: Woody Allen, Kathy Bates, Philip Bosco, John Cusack, Mia Farrow, Jodie Foster, Fred Gywnne, Robert Joy, Julie Kavner, Madonna, John Malkovich, Kenneth Mars, Kate Nelligan, Donald Pleasance, Wallace Shawn, Kurtwood Smith, Josef Sommer, David Ogden Stiers, Lily Tomlin
An Orion Pictures Release. Black and white. 105 minutes

Husbands and Wives (1992)
A Jack Rollins–Charles H. Joffe Production
Associate Producer: Thomas Reilly
Casting: Juliet Taylor
Co-Producers: Helen Robin, Joseph Hartwick
Editor: Susan E. Morse, A.C.E.
Production Designer: Santo Loquasto
Costume Designer: Jeffrey Kurland
Director of Photography: Carlo Di Palma, A.I.C.
Executive Producers: Jack Rollins, Charles H. Joffe
Producer: Robert Greenhut
Writer and director: Woody Allen
Cast: Woody Allen, Lysette Anthony, Blythe Danner, Cristi Conaway, Judy Davis, Mia Farrow, Timothy Jerome, Juliette Lewis, Liam Neeson, Sydney Pollack, Ron Rifkin, Jerry Zaks
A Tri-Star Release. Color. 108 minutes

Manhattan Murder Mystery (1993)
A Jack Rollins–Charles H. Joffe Production

Associate Producer: Thomas Reilly

Casting: Juliet Taylor

Co-Producers: Helen Robin, Joseph Hartwick

Editor: Susan E. Morse, A.C.E.

Production Designer: Santo Loquasto

Costume Designer: Jeffrey Kurland

Director of Photography: Carlo Di Palma, A.I.C.

Executive Producers: Jack Rollins, Charles H. Joffe

Producer: Robert Greenhut

Writers: Woody Allen and Marshall Brickman

Director: Woody Allen

Cast: Jerry Adler, Alan Alda, Woody Allen, Joy Behar, Angelica Huston, Diane Keaton, Ron Rifkin

A Tri-Star Release. Color. 108 minutes

Bullets Over Broadway (1994)

Sweetland Films

A Jean Doumanian Production

Associate Producer: Thomas Reilly

Casting: Juliet Taylor

Co-Producer: Helen Robin

Editor: Susan E. Morse, A.C.E.

Production Designer: Santo Loquasto

Costume Designer: Jeffrey Kurland

Director of Photography: Carlo Di Palma, A.I.C.

Co-Executive Producers: Jack Rollins, Charles H. Joffe, Letty Aronson

Executive Producers: Jean Doumanian, J.E. Beaucaire

Producer: Robert Greenhut

Writers: Woody Allen and Douglas McGrath

Director: Woody Allen

Cast: Jim Broadbent, John Cusack, Harvey Fierstein, Chazz Palminteri, Mary-Louise Parker, Rob Reiner, Jennifer Tilly, Tracey Ullman, Joe Viterelli, Jack Warden, Dianne Wiest

A Miramax Films Release. Color. 100 minutes

Don't Drink the Water (1994)

Editor: Susan E. Morse, A.C.E.

Production Designer: Santo Loquasto

Costume Designer: Suzy Benzinger

Director of Photography: Carlo Di Palma, A.I.C.

Co-Executive Producer: Letty Aronson

Executive Producers: Jean Doumanian, J.E. Beaucaire

Producer: Robert Greenhut

Writer: Woody Allen (based on his play)

Director: Woody Allen

Cast: Woody Allen, Erick Avari, Mayim Bialik, Dom DeLuise, Michael J. Fox, Edward Herrmann, Julie Kavner, Rosemary Murphy, Austin Pendleton, Josef Sommer, Robert Stanton

Aired on ABC Television Network. Color and black and white. 92 minutes

Mighty Aphrodite (1995)

Sweetland Films

A Jean Doumanian Production

Associate Producer: Thomas Reilly

Casting: Juliet Taylor

Co-Producer: Helen Robin

Editor: Susan E. Morse, A.C.E.

Production Designer: Santo Loquasto

Costume Designer: Jeffrey Kurland

Director of Photography: Carlo Di Palma, A.I.C.

Co-Executive Producers: Jack Rollins, Charles H. Joffe, Letty Aronson

Executive Producers: Jean Doumanian, J.E. Beaucaire

Producer: Robert Greenhut

Writer and director: Woody Allen

Cast: F. Murray Abraham, Woody Allen, Claire Bloom, Helena Bonham Carter, Kathleen Doyle, Olympia Dukakis, Danielle Ferland, Jimmy McQuaid, Peter McRobbie, Dan Moran, Dan Mullane, Steve Randazzo, Michael Rapaport, J. Smith-Cameron, Mira Sorvino, David Ogden Stiers, Jack Warden, Peter Weller

Color. 94 minutes

ACKNOWLEDGMENTS

Thanks to the following people: Ernest Boehm, my photo agent, for twenty-three years of loyalty and hard work on my behalf, and for his dedication and friendship; Anahid Markarian and Vincent Tcholakian of Diana Custom Photo Lab, for being two terrific people and for making, as always, excellent prints of my work; Lauren Gibson, for her help and good nature; Derrick Tseng, for his alert eye, his wonderful commentary, and his overall vision; Charles Champlin, for his keen observation of Woody; Paul Gottlieb, for giving this book the go-ahead and for his warm, avuncular manner, which has impressed me since we first met; Diana Murphy, for her superb work as my editor and for her patience with me; Carol Morgan, for her verve and her enthusiasm for all the work that went into making the book come to life; Dana Sloan, for her inventive design, which provides a handsome home for the photos; Shun Yamamoto, for maintaining Abrams's high production standards on this book; Jill Revson, for her help and good taste early on in the project; Ellen Harrington and the late Douglas Edwards, both of the Academy of Motion Picture Arts and Sciences, for their interest in my work and for organizing it into an exhibition; and, finally, Tania Themmen, for the great memories and for being my muse and *the* "slice" of my life.

Brian Hamill

INDEX